KAMA SUTRA

SEXUAL POSITIONS FOR HIM AND

FOR HER

ANNE HOOPER

DK

LONDON, NEW YORK, MUNICH,
MELBOURNE, AND DELHI

Designer	Carla De Abreu
Senior Editor	Peter Jones
Senior Designer	Helen Spencer
Brand Manager for Anne Hooper	Lynne Brown
Category Director	Corinne Roberts
US Editor	Margaret Parrish
DTP	Karen Constanti
Production	Kevin Ward
Jacket Editor	Carrie Love
Jacket Designer	Nicola Powling

First American Edition, 2004

Published in the United States by
DK Publishing, Inc.
375 Hudson Street
New York, New York 10014
04 04 06 07 08 10 9 8 7 6 5 4 3 2 1

A Cataloguing-in-Publication record for this
book is available from the Library of Congress.

ISBN 0-7566-0530-X

Color reproduction by GRB, Italy
Printed and bound in Singapore by Star Standard

Discover more at
www.dk.com

CONTENTS FOR HER

Introduction *for her*

Pocket versions of the Kama Sutra have been slipped under pillows, into Christmas stockings, or given as Valentine and engagement presents. So what is it about this particular book that still intrigues?

The answer has to lie in the fascinating mix of exotic sensual experience and lavishly illustrated images that encompass both the ancient and the modern editions. There is something timeless and enduring about this particular work of sensuality, giving it a prestige many modern sex books do not possess. The world-famous words produce a heady mix when combined with dazzling yet sensitive photographs of loving couples. Somehow this book illustrates the famous sex positions without causing offense. And ultimately the Kama Sutra aims to satisfy our curiosity about one of the most profound aspects of our existence—human sexuality in all its glory.

Anne J. Hooper

KAMA SUTRA

SEXUAL POSITIONS FOR HIM AND

FOR HER

ANNE HOOPER

KAMA SUTRA

for her

Kama Sutra background for her

Although the original Kama Sutra was aimed at men, women are not neglected in the text. There are many pages detailing how male lovers can excite female sensuality.

These details include many different types of kisses and touch, plus a number of sexual positions that women may initiate. The original manuscript was actually a collection of ancient Sanskrit writings on the art of love and sexual technique. They were collated some time between the first and fourth centuries AD by a Brahman called Vatsyayana. Brahmans were Indian noblemen and scholars who believed that life consisted of *dharma*, *artha*,

and *kama*. *Dharma* was the acquisition of religious merit; *artha* was the acquisition of wealth; and *kama* was the acquisition of love or sensual pleasure.

Helping women take the initiative

Of special interest to women in the *Kama Sutra* are the "women on top" forms of lovemaking. Vatsyayana recommends that these be used when the woman seeks some satisfaction but her man is

overtired. He also recommends that if a woman "sees her lover is fatigued by constant congress, without having his desire satisfied, she would, with his permission, lay him down upon his back, and give him assistance by acting his part. She may also do this to satisfy the curiosity of her lover or her own desire for novelty."

The subtleties of wooing

A relaxed but curious state of mind is a special prerequisite for many women. The *Kama Sutra* excels in the advice given to young male suitors on how to woo their future lovers. This advice ranges from present-giving and childish games extending right on through to sitting her upon his knee and stroking and cajoling her.

Arousing your woman

No other sex manual pays so much attention to the lead-in to good sex as the *Kama Sutra*. By this I refer to the detailed chapters on stroking, shampooing, grooming, many different styles of kissing, even right down to scratching and biting. All of these are grist for Vatsyayana's sensual mill where women are concerned. He understands that women often need different arousal factors than men and in teaching these techniques to his male students, Vatsyayana is doing women of all times and ages a wonderful favor!

WIDELY OPENED

In this position, where you
arch your back so that
your pelvis moves up to join
that of your partner, you can
make it very clear how eager
you are for penetration.
As you lean back on your
elbows you will gain the
perfect opportunity to gaze
into your lover's face and
watch his excitement.
Face-to-face positions
like this can be emotionally
arousing, although this one
is extremely tiring so don't
expect to last too long.
It can last for as long as
you can keep your back
curved. Avoid it if you suffer
from a bad back.

CRAB'S POSITION

To get into this pleasurable position, bend
your knees and draw your thighs to your
stomach (like a crab retracting its claws).
When "letting go" playfully in positions
like this, we get to know each other's

*"He should gather from her
actions what she enjoys."*

KAMA SUTRA

innermost feelings, and likes and dislikes.
By bending and drawing back your knees
you make the muscles in your upper thighs
contract. Every push your partner makes on
your knees transfers to the thighs and to the
genital area, so that each thrust heightens
your pelvic tension and enjoyment.

RISING POSITION

In this position you need to raise your feet up straight above your man's shoulders so that he can kneel in front of you and introduce his penis into your vagina. By keeping your thighs pressed together, you do most of the work, producing exquisite

"Increase your love with the effects of gently marking the body with the nails."
KAMA SUTRA

sensations for both partners. By using the pressure of your thighs to squeeze the penis, you can increase the friction between the vagina and penis and heighten the intensity of your—and his—sexual excitement.

SIDE-BY-SIDE CLASPING

This loving embrace is reassuring and sensual, especially if there is any anxiety associated with sex. The act of simply wrapping yourself lovingly around your partner generates feelings of comfort and tenderness. The *Kama Sutra* suggests that the man lie on his left side and the

woman on her right, but these days we aren't so prescriptive. Choose whichever feels comfortable for you. In this intimate position you will each feel both protected and protective. Your senses will come alive as your skin is stroked, enabling you to relax and begin slow, unhurried love.

TWINING POSITION

Weaving and twining yourself around your partner forms part of the intricate, unspoken choreography of love, and enables you to get as close to each other as humanly possible. Such full-body touch and friction inevitably triggers feelings of powerful sexual excitement for both of you. The Twining Position requires you to place one leg across your lover's thigh in order to draw him as close to you as possible. As your excitement increases, the breast tissue in both of you swells, sometimes creating a red flush across the chest area.

THE PAIR OF TONGS

With your knees bent, you face your man, sitting astride him as he lies on his back. You draw his penis into you and repeatedly squeeze it with the muscles of your vagina, holding it tight for a long time. Penetration in this position is deep. By sitting astride your man you can stimulate yourself as well as him. If he doesn't wish to be totally passive, he can use his hands to stroke and caress you or use his fingers to stimulate your clitoris, or you can do so yourself.

THE TOP

This position is presumably included in the *Kama Sutra* as a joke. My advice is to steer clear of it. According to Vatsyayana, the movement requires some dexterity and is achieved only with practice. While sitting astride your partner, you raise your legs clear of his body and swivel around on his penis. As you perform this maneuver you should take care not to lose your balance, otherwise you may hurt yourself and your partner. Although just about feasible in theory, in reality this position is difficult and hazardous.

SUSPENDED CONGRESS

Your man leans against a wall and lifts you up by locking his hands underneath your buttocks or holding your thighs. You need to grip him with your legs as if riding a horse, and may need to facilitate his moves of thrusting forward and backward. If it is hard for your man to keep a sensual rhythm going, increase your pleasure by pushing off from the wall with your feet. This will give you more

"The woman should squeeze her internal muscles so that she pleasures her man."
KAMA SUTRA

support and help to maintain the rhythm of lovemaking. Clearly this is not a position for the over-voluptuous in figure since your man will require a lot of strength to pull you to him and then relax in sequential moves.

ANANGA RANGA

for her

Ananga Ranga background for her

*The Ananga Ranga **shares with the** Kama Sutra **the felicity
of being one of several books discovered, translated, and
published by the famous Victorian explorer Sir Richard Burton.***

Under the auspices of his
audacious Kama Shastra
Society, Burton and his
colleague Forster Fitzgerald
Arbuthnot dared risk the
opprobrium of decent Victorian
society in bringing these
ancient erotic classics to
contemporary times, publishing
the *Ananga Ranga* two years
after the *Kama Sutra*. The title
of the book, *Ananga Ranga,*
means "Stage of the Bodiless
One," which refers to the
moment when the Hindu
god of love, Kama, became

a bodiless spirit, while his
physical body was burned to a
pile of ashes by a stare from the
third eye of the great god Siva.

Eastern erotic refinement
But while the *Kama Sutra* was
written for lovers, married or
otherwise, this second book,
compiled in 1172, when
Indian society had become
more ordered than in the time
of the *Kama Sutra*, was written
to protect marriage from the
tedium that can so easily set
in. The book was written

shortly before the start of the Crusades, the great medieval religious wars that took place in the Middle East. European women of that time had a lot to be grateful to the Crusades for, if only they had known it. The journeying knights, their husbands, many of whom lived like kings in their conquered Moorish domains, brought back with them such Eastern erotic refinements as cleanliness and sexual foreplay.

Better sex for women

It is perfectly possible that these knights, many of whom lived abroad for years, were familiar with the *Ananga Ranga* itself and most certainly with its tenets. From the little we know of it, sex had previously been a pretty brutish activity. Men showed little knowledge of how women's sexuality worked and no understanding of any of the erotic refinements that make love memorable.

Sexual security

But back from the religious wars the newly sophisticated knights instigated such new-fangled systems as bath houses and regular changes of clothing. It is highly likely that they also instigated a variety and skill to lovemaking that their wives had not previously dreamed of. Since a knight could be all-powerful in his household, the fact that sex could be improved could well mean that the loving wife gained more security for herself.

ACCOMPLISHING POSITION

The Accomplishing Position is a natural follow-on to the Lotus Position. Leaning back on one hand for support and balance, you keep one of your legs lifted while making love. This makes for a different angle between the penis and vagina and alters the tension felt by both of you. This face-to-face position can be tender and loving as you can kiss your man and show him affection.

CRYING OUT POSITION

This position involves your man lifting you and moving you around on his penis. It works best when performed by a strong man and light woman. Your legs hang over your man's elbows, and he moves you from side to side—or forward and back in a variation known as the Monkey Position. This is a surprisingly arousing stroke for you since it puts pressure on a number of sensitive spots on the outer entrance of the vagina.

SNAKE TRAP

The name of this position
must refer to the fact that
since both lovers grasp
each other's feet there
is no escape. The snake is
trapped—inside the woman.
You sit in your man's lap
with your legs on either side
of him, while he sits with
his legs outstretched and
inserts his penis into you.
With your hands holding
on to each other's feet for
support, you both begin to
rock your pelvises to and
fro. This position is unlikely
to give you dynamite
sensation, but it will offer
you a lot of fun.

RAISED FEET POSTURE

The *Ananga Ranga* describes this posture thus: lying on her back, the woman bends her legs at the knees and draws them back "as far as her hair." Her partner then enters her from a kneeling position. You can gain considerable pleasure by raising your hips so that your partner penetrates you at an angle in which his penis stimulates your highly sensitive G-spot. You may also like to encourage him to use his hands to caress you and fondle your breasts.

THE REFINED POSTURE

This position allows for the deepest penetration so far. You lie with your legs bent on either side of your man's hips. He raises you up by lifting your buttocks with his hands so that he can position you at the best angle in which to thrust into you very effectively. If you like the idea, ask your lover to gently lift your buttocks up and away from the anus and perineum to offer you erotic sensations. You may also prefer that he use his free hand to caress your face and body, which can be powerfully exciting for you.

KAMA'S WHEEL

This is not a position
that leads to fierce erotic
stimulation. Instead, it can
be used as a sort of sexual
meditation. You sit astride
your lover with your legs
extended. Your man sits with
his legs outstretched and
grasps you securely behind
your shoulder blades. Both
your outstretched limbs
create a spokelike pattern
that gives the position its
name. Ideally you should be
able to lean back and move
just enough to keep your
man's penis erect, thus
allowing both of you to
focus only on this erotic
moment and blot out
all other concerns.

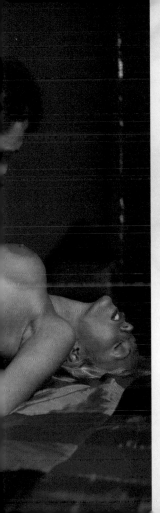

PLACID EMBRACE

As you lie on your back, your legs on either side of your man, he kneels before you and lifts your hips up to meet his penis. You can draw your man closer to you by crossing your ankles behind his back, emphasizing your feelings of tenderness and intimacy. As your man hugs you close to him, he can slip a pillow under your back so that you can thrust against him without hurting yourself, thus increasing the levels of pleasure for both of you.

CRAB EMBRACE

Side-by-side positions are great for those times when either partner is tired but still passionate, or when you are pregnant and do not want to put a lot of pressure on your abdomen. In the Crab Embrace, your man lies on his left side, placing his right thigh across your right thigh and

pulling you toward him. You place your left leg up over his buttocks and snuggle in close. As your man's right arm will be freed up, he can slide his hand up and down your back and buttocks with sensitive caresses as you make slow, unhurried love.

TRANSVERSE LUTE

To achieve this position you raise your leg slightly to
allow your partner to enter you, then he raises his leg and
rests it on your thigh. Side-by-side positions are good for
those men who need more friction during intercourse. The
penis thrusts are felt along the insides of your labia, which

are pressed against the penis by your outstretched legs.
These positions also give you an increased likelihood of
arousal and orgasm. Penetration will naturally pull on
one side of your vaginal opening and, if you are lying
on your left side, this can be especially stimulating.

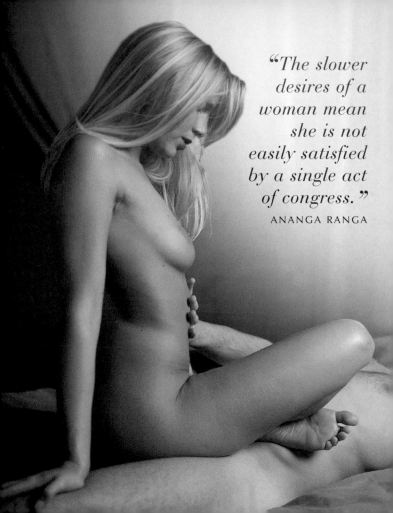

"The slower
desires of a
woman mean
she is not
easily satisfied
by a single act
of congress."

ANANGA RANGA

ASCENDING POSITION

Kalyana Malla describes in the *Ananga Ranga*, if a woman's "passion has not been gratified by previous copulation," she can sit cross-legged on her man's thighs, "seize" his penis, and insert it into her vagina and then move herself up and down. You can alter the angle of your partner's entry into your vagina to give yourself the stimulation you need to become highly aroused. This could be either clitoral stimulation from his penis, or from your own fingers as you rise and fall above him.

THE INVERTED EMBRACE

Your man lies back with you on top of him. You then insert his penis into your vagina, press your breasts to his, and move your hips. You can steady yourself by holding on to him. Being in control of the lovemaking will increase your excitement and allow you to absorb

yourself in the sensations that give you both pleasure. Your swiveling hips produce a kind of churning, side-by-side movement for your partner, like a vigorous body massage, that feels wonderful and different from the usual thrust of intercourse.

ORGASMIC ROLE-REVERSAL

In this position, you squat on your man's thighs, insert his penis, close your legs firmly, and adopt a churning motion so that you can "thoroughly satisfy" yourself. The freedom of movement that this position brings will give you control over the speed, angle, and amount by which you move your pelvis around. Add variety to your erotic sensations by varying the depth of penetration. This can be a useful method of intercourse when your partner is willing but tired.

PERFUMED GARDEN

for her

Perfumed Garden background for her

This North-African sex manual, originally written in the 16th century, resurfaced in the mid-1800s in Algeria, having been bought by a French officer who was stationed there.

This was the third book to be published by Sir Richard Burton's Kama Shastra Society. It was written in the 16th century by a character named Sheikh Nefzawi, who lived in what is now Tunisia and appears to have been a very early example of a sex therapist. His insights into sexual needs were rare and invaluable. Although the book was mainly written for men, it kept the sexual welfare of women clearly in mind. For the male-dominated culture of North Africa of that time, the *Perfumed Garden* provided enlightened subject matter.

The "ideal" woman

Nefzawi's own sexual preferences are vividly apparent when he describes the genital area of his "ideal woman." She needs "the lower part of the belly to be large, the vulva projecting and fleshy," and "the conduit to be narrow and not moist, soft to the touch and emitting a strong heat." The "not moist" reference emphasizes one of

the differences between Eastern and Western culture that continues today. Arabic women prefer to remain "dry," since they believe it makes intercourse sexier.

Genital character

By describing women's genitalia in great detail, Sheikh Nefzawi displays not just a sense of humor but also a recognition of something that many of us have lost sight of today. Just as all faces are different, so too are genitals—and personalities. The Sheikh uses these physical differences as a metaphor for the glorious variety within the nature of the female spirit. You can discern the supposed qualities of his women from the names he gives to their genitals alone! How about: the voluptuous, the crusher, the glutton, the beautiful, the hot one, and the delicious one?

Inspiring affection

In the *Perfumed Garden* Sheikh Nefzawi advised his male readers how to turn on their women. "Those things which develop the taste for coition are the toyings and touches which precede it, and then the close embrace at the moment of ejaculation! Believe me, the kisses, nibblings, and suction of the lips, the close embrace, the visits of the mouth to the nipples of the bosom, and the sipping of fresh saliva, these are the things to render affection lasting."

GRIPPING WITH TOES

This position is probably best used as a transition from one move to another, or as an interlude during more vigorous lovemaking. You lie on your back and your man kneels between your thighs, placing his hands on either side of your neck, and bracing himself with his toes to keep his balance. You may wrap your legs around his waist and pull yourself up on to his penis so that he can penetrate you fully. Although he is unable to thrust freely in this posture, he can vary the angle of penetration by leaning toward or away from you.

THE ONE WHO STOPS AT HOME

In this technique you can demonstrate how hot you are for your man. You lie on your back with your knees bent and your feet and shoulders supporting your weight.
Your man leans over you and supports himself on his hands and knees. You push up onto the balls of your feet and lift your hips to allow him to enter you, then drop your pelvis down suddenly.
You then lift and drop your pelvis in quick succession.

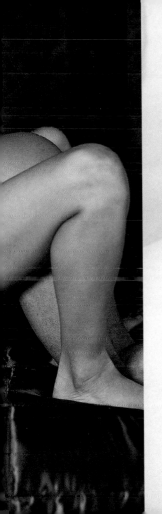

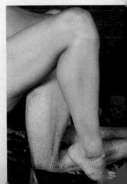

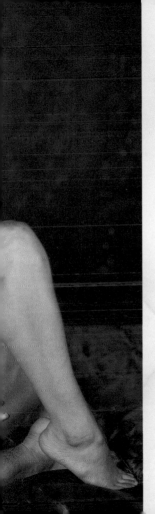

THIRD POSTURE

Your man kneels between your legs, then lifts your left leg up over his right shoulder and tucks the right leg under his left arm. He then penetrates you. Just the thought of this position can be very titillating to many women, but I recommend that you attempt it only when you are fully aroused. During sexual arousal the vagina undergoes a process called "tenting," in which the upper end enlarges so it can accommodate a deep-thrusting penis comfortably. You feel stretched wide open and may gain real pleasure from the experience.

FITTING ON OF THE SOCK

This is a terrific position for the woman. Your man uses his penis as a dildo to arouse you in preparation for deep penetration. Try it before other deep-thrusting positions. While you lie on your back with legs apart, he rests your buttocks on his thighs and inserts the tip of his penis into your vulva, which he then pulls closed gently with his thumb and first finger. He moves his penis back and forth sensitively to moisten the outer lips with his secretion before he penetrates you.

FOURTH POSTURE

Your partner kneels, and positions your legs over his shoulders, he then raises your hips slightly. This allows him to explore the most pleasurable angles of penetration. Your sexual response can immediately increase if the penis puts pressure on the "2 o'clock" and "10 o'clock" spots on your vagina. Initiate kissing, fondling, and stroking well before penetration in order to be properly aroused. During intercourse, you may climax from the powerful sensations created by the penis pressing against the different parts of your vaginal walls.

FIFTH POSTURE

Both lovers lie with their legs outstretched.
You rest your uppermost leg on top of
your man's leg, bending it a little to allow
him to enter you deeply. He pulls you
toward him by grasping your hip and
rolling you on to your side. By pulling you
and then letting go a little, he rocks
you on and off his penis.

LOVE'S FUSION

Many lovers feel aroused by the sheer sensation of entwining their legs. Here you hook your leg directly over your lover's hip so your vagina is wide open for penetration. If you are not feeling strong, this is an easy method of enjoying energetic intercourse. Move in rhythm with your partner's thrusting to increase your arousal.

RAINBOW ARCH

This is one of those crazy positions that couples fall into when fooling around. It has more novelty value than pleasurable profit, but you never know—it might turn out to be the most erotic experience of your life. Before penetration, your man lies at right angles to you, puts his legs between yours, then moves his legs around so that you can reach his feet. The unusual angle of entry provides novel sensations for you. You are literally touched from angles never otherwise experienced!

FROG FASHION

This intimate position feels friendly, even though neither partner can move very much. Your man holds on to your shoulders and pulls you forward onto his penis. He needs to push your knees back

"Visits of the mouth to the nipple give lasting affection."

PERFUMED GARDEN

gently so that your heels are close enough to your buttocks to allow him room for entry. You wrap your arms around your knees and lean back. Since your feet are tucked underneath his buttocks, you can lean back with a fair degree of comfort.

EIGHTH POSTURE

To perform the Eighth Posture you must be adept at yoga. You can lie back in one of two positions: either with your thighs open and your ankles crossed as though in the lotus position, while your man kneels astride you; or you can cross your legs and pull them back before he enters you, so your legs rest against his chest. Each of the variations of this cross-legged posture has its own benefits. Pull your crossed legs back for deep penetration and G-spot stimulation or cross your ankles for clitoral stimulation.

NINTH POSTURE

This position has three main variants—two rear-entry and one face-to-face. In the rear-entry versions you lie face down across a bed with your knees on the floor or stand and lean forward over the bed. In the face-to-face version, you lie on your back on a bed with your feet on the floor. All of these positions are easy to get out of should you be interrupted unexpectedly.

TENTH POSTURE

Despite appearances,
this is a position in which
the woman dominates.
You lie with your straight
legs parted and your man
kneels between your thighs.
You then lift your knees to
squeeze your lover around
the waist. At the same time
you reach above your head
with one or both hands and
grasp the headboard. Once
he has inserted his penis,
your man leans forward
to grasp your hands so that
you both move back and
forth with a seesaw motion.
Movement for both partners
is limited, but since you are
in control your man must
respond to your rhythms.

POUNDING ON THE SPOT

This position will feel strangely familiar to any woman who is used to horseback riding. The movement of your thigh muscles is the same as that used for trotting! Your man sits with his legs outstretched, while you sit astride him facing him and guide his member into your vagina.

"Men deserve success with women eager to please."
PERFUMED GARDEN

This position allows you to be in control— and power is, after all, an aphrodisiac. Use your vaginal muscles to grip your lover's penis as you move up and down to generate further excitement for yourself.

RECIPROCAL SIGHTS OF THE POSTERIOR

Your partner lies on his back, ideally with his head propped up by a pillow so that he can get a pleasing view of your buttocks as you rise and fall above him. You sit astride your man in any way that pleases you, provided you have your back to him. You can turn your head and body slightly so that you, too, can see your posterior rising and falling. Your balance is best maintained by leaning forward slightly during lovemaking.

INTERCHANGE OF COITION

This is another of Sheikh Nefzawi's suggestions for "women acting the part of a man." Your partner lies on his back with his legs open, a pillow between his thighs. This is a sophisticated version of a push-up, whereby you lever yourself up and down, your vagina and thighs tightly gripping your man's penis. By varying the angle of thrust slightly and moving your pelvis close up against your partner's you can ensure clitoral stimulation.

BELLY TO BELLY

There is a place in every couple's sex life for erotic immediacy, so show the strength of your attraction to each other by being impulsive and abandoned. Here, each partner stands with their feet firmly on the floor or, if it feels more natural, you hook one leg over his thigh. This enables you to move up and down as you take it in turns to thrust, each alternately thrusting against the other and

"The two orgasms take place simultaneously, and enjoyment comes to the man and woman together."
PERFUMED GARDEN

then withdrawing. Most of the action comes from your partner, but he can help by supporting you in his arms, even lifting you if this feels desirable. The immediate passion and intensity of your lovemaking will make you both feel blissfully aroused.

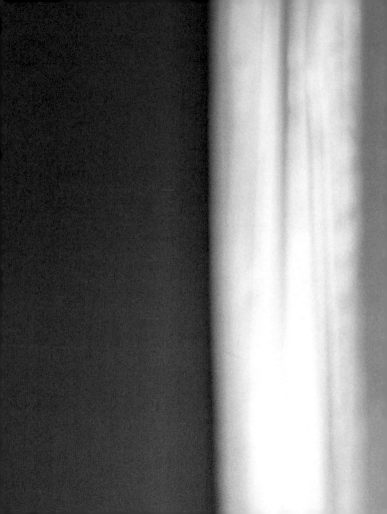

THE TAO

for her

The Tao *background for her*

At the heart of the Tao, a collection of ancient Chinese writings, is the belief that ulitmate harmony exists in the universe, and this can be attained by following the way of the Tao.

The word "Tao" means "path," but in Taoism it also signifies the functioning of the universe. Animating all that exists in the entire universe are twin forces: Yin, which is negative, passive, and nourishing; and Yang, which is positive, active, and consuming. The major component of a woman's nature is seen as Yin. However, an inbalance of Yin and Yang exists between the sexes, so that the woman needs the male force to balance her. These forces are exchanged by sexual union, and it is at orgasm that they are at their most potent.

Climax like a flower

Orgasm, therefore, is of supreme importance in the practice of Tao and a woman's orgasm is likened to a flower, uncurling from the center, blooming in the sun as petal after petal unfolds. Inside herself she opens up entirely and surrenders to the man who can take her at any pace and bring her to the most intense ecstasy.

Eastern orgasms

In addition the *Tao* teaches us that the Eastern concept of orgasm goes much further than the Western one. It describes a woman's orgasm as a series of upward-rising steps followed by one declining step. These steps flow together with some degree of overlap, building on the experience of each previous step. The woman therefore experiences many levels of opening to sensation until she is finally completely exposed to the man who is her server.

The nine levels of orgasm

There are nine levels in all, the first four corresponding pretty much to the levels that Westerners understand, namely heavy breathing, passionate kissing, passionate embracing, and a series of vaginal spasms accompanied by a flow of vaginal fluids.

During level five, however, the woman's joints begin to loosen and she may bite her partner. In level six she undulates like a snake, wrapping her arms and legs around him. In level seven her blood is "boiling" and she tries to touch her man everywhere. At level eight her muscles relax totally. At level nine she collapses in a "little death" and feels completely opened up. The Tao of Sex is one of eight pillars of Taoist wisdom and Taoist sexology aims to improve health, harmonize relationships, and increase spiritual realization.

GALLOPING HORSE

This position requires your man to hold on to your neck and foot like a bareback rider clinging to a speeding horse. He kneels between your legs with his thighs beneath your buttocks. You bend your knees to grasp him with your thighs and tuck your feet in close to his. After he has entered you he holds the back of your neck with one hand, pulls your foot or ankle close to him with the other hand and begins to thrust. Avoid this position if your man is tall and you are small. It could prove to be impossible, or dangerous if he loses his balance.

MANDARIN DUCKS

Mandarin ducks mate for life and so are considered lovebirds and symbols of marriage in China. Here, you lie on your back with your right leg stretched out. Leaning over slightly to the right you bend your left knee and raise your leg. Your partner faces you and sits on top of your thighs. He rests his weight on his left leg by kneeling on the bed or squatting. He then bends his right knee and moves his right leg forward under your raised left leg. As he does so he penetrates you.

HORSE CROSS FEET

The title refers to a horse's legs appearing to cross over as it gallops. The crossing of the woman's hand and knee give such an impression. You lie on your back and bend your right knee while your man kneels in front of you and leans over you. He steadies himself by putting his weight on his right hand just by your left shoulder. He clasps your right ankle with his left hand and, drawing you close, penetrates you. He then thrusts fast to gain the sensation of galloping

DRAGON TURN

To the ancient Chinese, the long limbs and flexible bodies displayed in this position resembled the mythical dragon. The woman's knees and elbows do, indeed, convey the impression of dragon wings. You lie on your back with your legs bent at the knees. Your hands hold each knee wide apart, and you lift your feet up high so that your heels rest on your man's hips as he kneels on either side of your buttocks. He supports himself on his hands so that he can penetrate you and begins alternating deep and shallow thrusts.

BUTTERFLIES IN FLIGHT

The movements of the woman's outstretched arms, or
wings, in this evocative position are perhaps like those of
a fluttering butterfly. You lie on top of your lover, and once
you have lowered yourself on to his penis both of you
stretch your arms out to either side and hold hands.

Push your toes against your man's feet to move up and
down and increase the sexual friction. This will provide
thrilling sensations as his penis moves inside your vagina.
This position is particularly suitable when you want to
assume the dominant role and make love to your man.

CAT AND MOUSE SHARING A HOLE

This is a straightforward love position in which you lie full length along your partner's body with your knees on either side of his thighs and your hands supporting your weight. Strenuous effort is required if either partner is to reach orgasm like this, but your striving together can be mutually exciting. Despite its evocative title, I find this a disappointing version of the love position. My own choice would include active stimulation by the hands and fingers, which can stand in as "mice."

BUTTERFLY

This position resembles a butterfly, not so much by its shape as by the woman's movements. You sit on your lover's hips, insert his penis into your vagina, and lean back on your hands, which you place on his legs. You then use your legs to raise your hips up and down on his penis slowly. It is the movement of your body, with your knees jutting high, that resembles a butterfly in flight. This role-reversal position may serve to heighten each partner's erotic desires.

BIRDS FLY BACK ON BACK

This position can be interpreted as two mating birds in
flight, although it takes quite a stretch of the imagination
to see it! Your man lies on his back and, with your back to
him, you lower yourself onto him in a sitting position and
carefully insert his penis into your vagina. You then drop
your head and lean forward slightly. Position your weight
over your feet, grasp your ankles or knees, and raise and
lower yourself on his penis using your thigh muscles.

SINGING MONKEY

In this position the woman sits in her lover's lap and curls herself around him as if she were a monkey clinging to him. You lean back on your outstretched hand to lever your pelvis up and down in a type of thrusting motion. Although both of you are restricted in your movements, you can caress each other's bodies and make eye contact, creating an intimate tenderness between you.

JADE JOINT

The process of carving and joining together two pieces of jade to form a jade joint, or jade cross, is considered an art form in China. To replicate this revered pattern, you lie on your left side and bend your right leg at the knee, pulling it up to hip level with your right hand. Your man kneels behind your hips, holds your right leg up and across him, while penetrating you deeply. By pulling your leg right back, you stretch the vaginal area, which makes you feel exposed, vulnerable, and sensuous. This will be an erotic turn-on for you both.

TIGER STEP

One method of overcoming instability during love-making can be to adopt a posture where you rest your forearms and head on the ground. You begin in a kneeling position, then lower your forearms and head to the ground so that your body is buttressed against your lover's vigorous thrusts as he kneels behind you. Since you support yourself in this position, your man does not have to hold up his body weight. This leaves his hands free to roam across your back, enlivening you with his touch and increasing your levels of arousal.

RABBIT GROOMING

This hunched-over position is reminiscent of a rabbit grooming itself. Your partner lies on his back while you sit on top of him, facing his feet. Your knees are bent as you lean forward slightly, keeping your hands on the ground. As you enclose your man, you move your hips in a circular motion— a little like hula-hooping. Some women find Rabbit Grooming difficult because it requires flexible knee joints and strong leg muscles. But it's worth pursuing, since the circular movement of your hips creates many unusual and wonderful sensations.

TURTLE MOVE

The languid dog-paddle motion of a turtle afloat in tropical seas can be mimicked by the twin movements of penetration and withdrawal in this position. Your man should pull his penis out almost entirely at the end of each stroke, while you alternately pull back and push forward.

PINE TREE

This is another position where you lie on your back with your legs raised and resting on your partner's shoulders. The shape of your straight legs is thought to resemble a straight-growing pine tree. You hold your kneeling partner around the hips while he places his hands around your waist and then penetrates you.

Index *for her*

ACKNOWLEDGEMENTS

The publisher would like to thank the following for their kind permission to reproduce their photographs:
10-11, 30-31, 58-59: © Christie's Images Ltd; **92-93:** © akg-images
All other images © Dorling Kindersley
For further information see: **www.dkimages.com**
DK would like to thank **Laurence Errington** for the index.

KAMA
SUTRA
SEXUAL POSITIONS FOR HER AND
FOR HIM
ANNE HOOPER

KAMA
SUTRA

SEXUAL POSITIONS FOR HER AND

FOR HIM

ANNE HOOPER

DK

LONDON, NEW YORK, MUNICH,
MELBOURNE, AND DELHI

Designer	Carla De Abreu
Senior Editor	Peter Jones
Senior Designer	Helen Spencer
Brand Manager	
for Anne Hooper	Lynne Brown
Category Director	Corinne Roberts
US Editor	Margaret Parrish
DTP	Karen Constanti
Production	Kevin Ward
Jacket Editor	Carrie Love
Jacket Designer	Nicola Powling

First American Edition, 2004

Published in the United States by
DK Publishing, Inc.
375 Hudson Street
New York, New York 10014
04 04 06 07 08 10 9 8 7 6 5 4 3 2 1

A Cataloguing-in-Publication record for this
book is available from the Library of Congress.

ISBN 0-7566-0530-X

Color reproduction by GRB, Italy
Printed and bound in Singapore by Star Standard

Discover more at
www.dk.com

CONTENTS FOR HIM

Introduction *for him*

Two thousand years ago, at the time the Kama Sutra was first written, in order to become fully rounded citizens, men were supposed to number amongst their many skills the ability to be fabulous lovers.

Even though we now live in the 21st century, that belief has not changed. Naturally this edition of the manual has been brought right up to date so that today's lovers can relate to it, but the world-famous love positions remain the same. I have even tried to retain the flavor of the original English translation because the Victorian language of the time was so descriptive, attaining erotic meaning all of its own. Above all, the original author, Vatsyayana, knew that the key to really good lovemaking was to take things slowly and sensuously.

Anne J. Hooper

KAMA
SUTRA

for him

Kama Sutra background for him

The Kama Sutra is a collection of Sanskrit writings, collected by Brahman Vatsyayana, some time between the first and fourth centuries AD to help young men become wonderful lovers.

It was considered important that men should learn skillful emotional and tactile sex techniques because Kama (the acquisition of love and sensual pleasure) was a cornerstone of the qualities that went into the makeup of the complete and successful male. The original text makes it clear that there are several types of sexual behavior open to men of that period. Special techniques include, for example, the wooing of very young girls, because these are their future wives. Most of these techniques work perfectly well with older women, too!

Gaining sexual experience
However, the *Kama Sutra* also recognized that men were likely to have lovers other than their wives. So instructions were given for pleasuring a courtesan or even for seducing other men's wives! Men's sexual vulnerability was recognized and many of the famous sex positions are suggested with

extra friction for the male member in mind or for easier penetration if mild impotence was a problem.

Sex magic

Nor were more extreme measures omitted if the male reader was experiencing bad luck in the bedroom. The *Kama Sutra* also includes magic spells and incantations to vanquish rivals who look to threaten your love success. And some of the most poisonous concoctions imaginable are described in the original text. They include, described in loving detail, actual recipes for lotions that you ate (ugh), put on your intimate parts (aagh), or even buried in the ground (on the principle that the burial of the potions would make you feel better).

Invaluable sex positions

But it is those famous sex positions for which this classic and most enduring of erotic texts is famous. A high congress position, for example, such as the Wife of Indra (page 17) enables a man with a small penis to achieve maximum penetration with a woman who has a large vagina. Low congress, such as the Twining Position (page 20, For Her section) allows a man with a large penis to penetrate a woman with a small vagina. There are reasons for the entire range of extraordinary positions, even if the object is just one of having a lot of fun.

YAWNING POSTURE

What begins as a straight-forward man-on-top position can evolve very easily into the Yawning Posture. By lifting her legs and opening her thighs, your partner enables you to place your knees on either side of her hips and lean gently against her to thrust. Looking down, you are able to see powerful sexual emotion on your lover's face. Although your movement is impeded by the barrier of her thighs, remember that not all erotic stimulation is about localized genital friction. Good sex includes the idea of sex as well as the actuality.

LOTUS–LIKE POSITION

To get into this position your partner crosses her legs and draws them up toward her torso before you lean over to penetrate her. This position may be a joke; since the strain imposed on the limbs makes it unlikely to be pleasurable. The few who can meet such a challenge may find it hard to sustain such a difficult position for very long, and the tangle of limbs beneath you may make it difficult to maintain your stroke. There's also a serious possibility of getting kicked in super-sensitive parts— assuming you're able to get anywhere near your goal!

VARIANT YAWNING

This is a satisfying position for you because it combines the ease of the missionary position with deeper penetration, though it may also be tiring because you support your weight on your arms. With the calves of her legs resting on your shoulders, your woman can hold her legs high in the air, adding an element of powerful eroticism for both of you.

WIFE OF INDRA

The position, named after Indrani, wife
of the Hindu god Indra, is mentioned in
the *Kama Sutra* as being suitable for the
"highest congress"—in which the vagina
is fully open to allow for maximum
penetration. Hold on to your partner's
thighs to control your thrusts.

SPLITTING OF THE BAMBOO

This acrobatic position calls for the woman to fold and unfold her legs during intercourse, and so requires considerable suppleness. The sequence is repeated again and again: your woman raises one leg and puts it on your shoulder; then, after a while, she brings that leg down and raises the other. Thus she "splits the bamboo." As your woman takes turns raising each leg, your penis is squeezed first by one set of vaginal muscles and then another, producing some very unusual sensations!

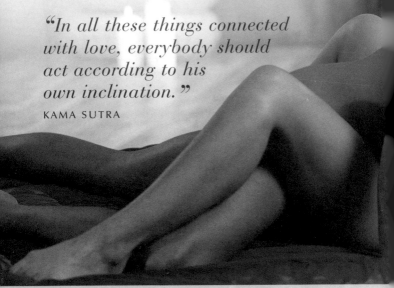

"In all these things connected with love, everybody should act according to his own inclination."

KAMA SUTRA

PRESSING POSITION

Here, your partner grips you with her thighs so that her vagina and pelvic muscles tighten around your penis. There's nothing easier than sliding into intercourse in this position. Value the body contact that Pressing offers, for in terms of arousal you really come alive. As you react

to your partner's intimate touch, your skin will tingle and the tension in the muscles mounts. The more you caress each other's skin and roll around, the greater the sexual charge. The woman can maintain the pressure in this position by following her partner's movements.

ELEPHANT POSTURE

Vatsyayana suggests seeking inspiration from the mating habits of other members of the animal kingdom. Imaginative lovers greatly extend their repertoire and gain an extra eroticism in their lovemaking. In this position, inspired by the mating techniques of elephants, the idea of you entering your partner from the rear can be thrilling. You can rear up from her with the small of your back arched inward as you thrust deeply. The animalistic power this affords you should add to your excitement.

CLASPING POSITION

Due to the frantic pace of our lives in the 21st century,
modern lovers may need to learn the value of slow,
languid lovemaking, of simply sliding in and out of
a lover's embrace. With legs and arms intertwined,
this position offers full body-to-body contact, encouraging

an intense, passionate embrace. The emphasis here is on closeness, and only a little movement should be necessary to enable you to sustain your erection. Your partner should hold you tight for you both to gain the most physical and emotional pleasure from this passive position.

MARE'S POSITION

A woman in control doesn't
have to be a dominatrix. Her
movements can be used to
nurture her man. The Mare's
Position is not an animal-
inspired posture, but instead
describes the maternal side
of lovemaking, where the
female takes care of the male.
It is more a technique than
a position, in which the
woman uses her vaginal
muscles to squeeze the penis
repeatedly, as if milking it.
Suggest the Mare's Position
to your woman if you are
feeling unwell, tired, or if
you just want a change.

HALF–PRESSED POSITION

This balletic position looks like a movement in a gymnastics routine. Your partner stretches one leg out past your body and bends the other leg at the knee, placing the sole of her foot on your chest. This action exposes her clitoris enough to give her the chance of clitoral stimulation.

PRESSED POSITION

Your woman draws her legs up and places both feet on your chest to achieve this submissive position. Like the Half-Pressed Position, you must be careful not to thrust too hard into her shortened vagina. You will feel very aroused by her vulnerability and the sense of your own strength.

THE SWING

This is an uncomplicated
woman-on-top position.
Your partner sits with her
back to you and swings
forward and backward
by bending her elbows up
and down, consecutively
covering and uncovering
your penis as she moves.
The swinging movements
of your woman across the
head of your penis are
especially sensual for you.
She will need to learn to
judge how far forward she
can swing before your penis
slips out of her vagina.

THE SUPPORTED CONGRESS

When passion suddenly overwhelms us, we may want spontaneous sex standing in the nearest available private space. Lovers can achieve this position by leaning against a wall or into one another. If your woman is much shorter than you, you can bend your knees or she can stand on

"As a couple, even talking about embracing can increase the strength of your desire."
KAMA SUTRA

your feet or on tiptoe. This is not guaranteed to work if there is a major height difference. The position can be an outrageously exciting one for you. Because you are supported by the wall or braced against your woman, you can thrust freely and passionately. If your woman lifts her thigh up against yours you can achieve greater penetration as you thrust, which will enhance the enjoyment of both partners.

CONGRESS OF A COW

In this challenging position your partner bends over and places one or both hands on the ground for support. You then "mount" her from behind to penetrate her. You need to hold her hard against you so that you can pull her backward and forward. This move allows for deep

"Passion alone gives birth to all the acts of the parties."
KAMA SUTRA

penetration and enables you to control the depth and power of your thrusts for maximum pleasure. To improve your partner's experience move your fingers around to her clitoris and stroke it in rhythm with your thrusting.

ANANGA
RANGA

for him

Ananga Ranga background for him

The Ananga Ranga *shares similarities with the* Kama Sutra, *since both draw on the same ancient Sanskrit scripts. However, they were written many centuries apart.*

By the time the *Ananga Ranga* appeared (around AD 1172), Indian society had become more ordered since Vatsyayana's time and extramarital sex was now censured. Author Kallyana Malla understood that the familiarity of sex with the same person led to sexual boredom. His desire was to prevent men from straying and incurring their wives' displeasure.

Keeping her sweet
If he was an educated man or merchant this was particularly important, for the lady of the house (or castle) played a major role in running the household and sharing in whatever business may have been conducted there. Women of the time directed the growing and cooking of food, organizing staff, making medicine and treating the sick, as well as being responsible for the welfare of the immediate household and all dependents living nearby. The man of the house risked a great deal by upsetting his wife.

Make sex varied

Stated Kallyana Malla: "The chief reason for separation between the married couple and the cause, which drives the husband to the embraces of strange women, and the wife to the arms of strange men, is the want of varied pleasures, and the monotony that follows possession."

It's classified!

He classified men and women by temperament and the size, smell, and taste of their sexual organs. Of women he wrote:

• "The Padmini Woman is fine, tender, and fair as the Lotus—her vaginal secretion is perfumed like the lily that has newly burst."

• "The Chitrini Woman is of middle size with hard, full breasts, well-turned thighs, and heavily made hips—her vaginal secretion is hot and perfumed like honey."

• "The Shankini Woman is of bilious temperament and her vaginal secretion is distinctly salty."

• "The Hastini Woman has a stout coarse body and walks with a slouching gait—her vaginal secretion tastes like the sweat from an elephant's brow[!]"

No prizes for guessing which of Kallyana Malla's types most women would choose to be!

LOTUS POSITION

Despite its yogalike name, the Lotus Position isn't that difficult to do. It does call for a lot of strength, since you will need to use your arms to help your woman move up and down on your penis. She sits on your knee, carefully lowering herself on to your penis, then extends her legs out behind you. Experiment with the most comfortable position for her legs; if she prefers to initiate the action herself instead of being subject to you moving her body, she will probably find that a kneeling position works best.

PAIRED FEET POSITION

In this position your partner lowers herself down on to your penis as you sit with your legs wide apart. Once they are in position and you have penetrated her fully, you press her thighs together with your hands while you thrust into her. You can increase the pleasurable sensations of your penis being squeezed by your woman's constricted vagina if you keep her thighs pressed together. Face-to-face positions like this can be especially arousing emotionally.

LEVEL FEET POSTURE

The *Ananga Ranga* positions in which the woman lies on her back as the man kneels to enter her are known as *uttana-bandha*. She feels an erotic sense of helplessness as he moves her to penetrate her deeply. Here, your partner lies on her back and you raise her body so her buttocks rest on your thighs. You brace yourself against her and position her legs on your shoulders, grasp her waist, and pull her up on to your penis. Because your woman's buttocks are raised you can penetrate her deeply, which will be highly pleasurable for you.

INTACT POSTURE

The Intact Posture is a position where the woman is physically confined and the man is in control. She lies on her back with her legs bent in close to her body and her knees resting on her chest. Your knees are positioned outside her thighs and you need to put one hand under her buttocks to lift her slightly before entering her. This is a relatively easy position from which to thrust and enjoy making love to your partner.

GAPING POSTURE

This is another dominant position in which you can thrust effectively while keeping your hands free to heighten your partner's pleasure. Pillows or cushions are used to arch your woman's back and raise her up to the required height to meet you. Her clitoris is stretched and exposed at this height and angle, and is therefore more likely to be affected by the thrust and pull of intercourse. You kneel between your lover's legs and, with your hands underneath her buttocks, pull her forward on to your erect penis.

THE ENCIRCLING POSITION

There are associations with bondage in this pose, which, combined with the fact that your woman's pelvis is opened wide and her clitoris exposed, creates a risqué feeling that is very exciting. Your woman lies with her calves crossed while you lean over to enter her. Your partner's openness will arouse your subconscious desires while you make love in this position, despite you not being able to penetrate too deeply.

SPLITTING POSTURE

As your woman lies with her legs in the air, you enter her from a kneeling position. You then lift her legs higher to rest them against your shoulder and begin to thrust. Meanwhile, she presses her knees and thighs together to constrict your penis. Positions such as this, where penetration is deep and the vagina is squeezed, are excellent if you are older and need a robust sensation during intercourse. Your penis feels tight inside the vagina, while the gripping sensation of your lover's thighs gives you additional friction.

PERFUMED GARDEN

for him

Perfumed Garden *background for him*

This book was written by a character named Sheikh Nefzawi, who was believed to have lived in what is now Tunisia during the 16th century and wanted to share his sexual expertise.

The Sheikh believed that men who deserved to succeed with women were those who were "anxious to please them." In his opinion, the ideal male possessed "a member that grows, gets strong, vigorous, and hard" when close to a woman. "His member should be able to reach the end of the canal of the female and completely fill it in all its parts." In other words, the Sheikh believed that biggest was best—a hotly debated issue in the 21st century.

The nine positions

Each of the Sheikh's nine main sexual positions was included for special reasons. For example, the first posture was suggested for men with long penises to help them keep from hurting their partners. The second, which is not very comfortable for women, is nevertheless perfect for men suffering from short penis problems.

Arousal for him

He also included several positions that give men a very

deep penetration. He recognized the importance of this—understanding that the farther the penis continues to travel down the vagina, the more the head and coronal ridge (a highly sensitive area around the head of the penis) are stimulated.

Arousal for her

Nor did he lose sight of the fact that, at least at the start of penetration, the vagina remains partly closed all the way down to the cervix. So he taught men that their women need to be fully aroused before attempting deep penetration.

An early sex therapist

The Sheikh showed himself to be an early type of sex therapist when he recommended arousing the woman with thumb and forefinger during intercourse, sitting back during penetration to do this if necessary.

A cool sense of humor

In suggesting some of his sillier positions, the Sheikh also showed himself to possess a cool sense of humor. These can surely only be recommended for fun rather than for their serious orgasmic potential. And that's the value of the man, and of the book that has come down to us. He demonstrates in his *Perfumed Garden* that there are literally hundreds of different ways of using sex to get closer to heaven.

FIRST POSTURE

The *Perfumed Garden* describes 11 main poses that pay
special atttention to physical differences between men
and women. In this first position, if you have a long penis
you can adjust the depth of your thrusts to keep from
hurting your partner. Your woman lies on her back and

raises her knees, resting her legs across your thighs. Support your weight on your hands and knees so you can control your thrusting once you have entered her. Use your toes to push against the bed as you thrust so you can control the power and rhythm of your lovemaking.

SECOND POSTURE

This is one of the positions that the author of the *Perfumed Garden*, Sheikh Nefzawi, recommends for a man whose "member is a short one." Your woman lies on her back and raises her legs in the air. She draws her legs back and holds them apart with her hands, allowing you to lean over her and move in close to her genitals. You kneel by her hips and place your hands on either side of her head for support before entering her. You should find that in this position your partner's constricted vagina gives you added satisfaction.

THE STOPPERAGE

You kneel between your lover's hips, leaning forward against her bent legs, and pressing her knees toward her breasts. This pushes the cervix forward, making penetration fairly difficult. Once you have inserted your penis, it is pressed against the cervix, as if stopping up a bottle with a cork. Nefzawi warns that this position should be tried only by men with a short or soft penis to keep from hurting the woman. The walls of your lover's vagina are pressed together, bringing you an intensity of sensation and pleasure.

WITH LEGS IN THE AIR

With your partner lying on her back, take her legs up across your chest and rest them beside each other, on the same shoulder, as you penetrate her. You can also squeeze her buttocks together with your thighs so she is pressed hard on to your penis. If you are an older man who requires vigorous pressure on the penis to achieve or maintain arousal, this position will provide enough stimulation to bring you to climax. Alternate forceful thrusts with gentle ones for maximum pleasure.

TAIL OF THE OSTRICH

Intercourse is not as pleasurable in this position as in others, but the highly erotic experience of seeing your woman in this unusual posture may fulfill some of your sexual fantasies. Kneel by your woman's raised hips and lift her legs, holding them against your chest as you enter her. You can vary the sensations you feel by raising or lowering your lover's hips, which alters the depth and angle of penetration. As you do this, support the small of her back with your hand.

SIXTH POSTURE

This classic rear-entry position
may generate powerfully
atavistic feelings. Your
woman rests on her knees
and elbows and parts her legs
enough to allow you to kneel
between them. You draw her
backward on to your erection.
She can lower or heighten
her position to match your
height by leaning up or down
on her elbows and forearms.
This is a naturally pleasurable
position for you to thrust
deeply and achieve climax
as you gaze down at your
partner's buttocks and caress
her back.

COITUS FROM THE BACK

In this rear-entry position you lie flat on top of your partner's back. A pillow is placed underneath her pelvis to raise her hips, so that you can penetrate her deeply and prevent your penis from accidentally slipping out of her vagina.

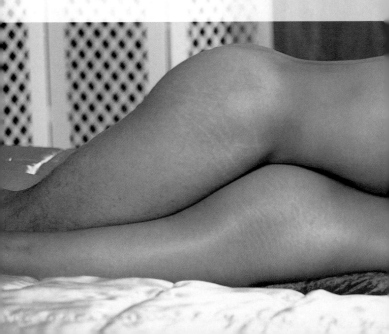

a 5

According to Sheikh Nefzawi, this is the easiest of all lovemaking methods. Your member is aligned with your partner's vagina in such a way as to ensure G-spot stimulation for her and a high level of arousal and deep penetration for both of you.

SEVENTH POSTURE

The Seventh Posture seems to favor the flexibility only really possessed by gymnasts. Sheikh Nefzawi specifies that your woman lie on her side, although the pose is marginally less difficult if she lies on her back. You sit back on your heels with one of her legs over your shoulder and the other between your thighs. Have fun exploring your own personal fantasies as you arouse each other and make love in this face-to-face position.

THE SEDUCER

This position has two versions. In the first, shown here, your woman wraps her legs around your waist to give you leverage as you thrust. In the second, which provides deeper penetration, she puts her legs over your shoulders. Ask your woman to guide your penis into her vagina so she can knead and massage it before insertion. This will give you a little extra stimulation before lovemaking in this sensual position begins.

ALTERNATIVE MOMENT OF PIERCING

You would need to be a flexible athlete with a very small partner to achieve this position successfully. Your woman sits between your knees so that you can both place the soles of your feet together. After penetration you move your partner back and forth on your penis instead of thrusting from the pelvis. You can do this by first pulling her toward you and then letting her drop back slightly, or, as Nefzawi suggests, she can sit on your feet which you then move backward and forward!

THE QUICKIE

Spontaneous sex features regularly in our lives in this speedy era. But it doesn't have to be second best. Just the idea of a stolen quickie can be extremely erotic. This profoundly tantalizing position, which can be performed clothed or naked, provides

"A man with a long member is relished by women."

PERFUMED GARDEN

immediate physical satisfaction, as you make the most of a few precious moments. The position is also easy to get out of should you be interrupted.

RACE OF THE MEMBER

You may enjoy heightened erotic thoughts as well as physical sensations in this role-reversal position. You lie with a large pillow under your shoulders and draw your knees up to form a V-shape. Your woman faces you, lowers herself down between your thighs, and inserts your penis into her vagina. In the advanced version, shown here, you pull your knees up toward your shoulders so your lover can sit astride your thighs and "ride" you. She needs to push herself up and down on your erect penis by bending her knees.

THE FITTER-IN

What you achieve with the Fitter-In is a living work of art. Your woman sits with her legs over your thighs. Then, with both of you being careful to maintain a mutually enjoyable rhythm, you grip each other's arms and rock gently backward and forward. The *Perfumed Garden* recommends that you maintain an exact rhythm "by the assistance of your heels which are resting rocking motion rather than a thrusting action provides just enough stimulation to prolong your erection.

ELEVENTH POSTURE

Your partner lies on her back to let you penetrate her. You lean over her, supporting your upper body weight on your hands to begin thrusting. The depth of penetration achieved creates intensely pleasurable stimulation for both partners. You will also have good control of your

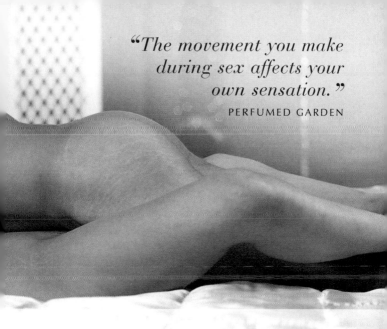

> *"The movement you make during sex affects your own sensation."*
>
> PERFUMED GARDEN

thrusting, allowing you to vary the pace and tempo so that your lovemaking can be long and drawn out or rapid and explosive. The movement of intercourse will pull your partner's labia rhythmically across her clitoris, creating a gentle friction that may trigger orgasm.

THE TAO

for him

The Tao *background for him*

The Tao is a collection of ancient Chinese wisdom that includes a complete world view. Taoists believe in following "the way" of The Tao and see life as a balance of opposites.

In this balance everything has an equal and opposite reaction. The twin forces of life, Yin and Yang, oppose each other. Yin indicates the negative, passive, and nourishing and is mainly feminine; Yang, the positive, active, and consuming and is mainly masculine. But each sex needs the other to balance the Yin and Yang between them perfectly.

Sexual energy points

Taoist thinkers advocate that sexual stimulation should be protracted in order to reach the highest levels of arousal. This is not just for sensual pleasure; its main purpose is to promote sexual health and energy and increase spiritual realization.

One Tao exercise directed especially at men asks you to see the interior of the vagina and the exterior of the penis as full of high-energy points. Logically this means that the more you massage each of them, the greater your sexual well-being will be.

The Sets of Nine

This is a Tao exercise designed to massage you into well-being through intercourse. The man practices a series of deep and shallow strokes. So in phase one he thrusts only the penis head into the vagina before withdrawing. He does this shallow stroke nine times, and then thrusts the entire penis into the vagina once. He follows this with eight shallow strokes and two deep ones. Then seven shallow strokes and three deep ones. Right on down to one shallow stroke followed by nine deep ones. This constitutes a Set of Nine

Injaculation

Unique to Tao sex instruction is the notion of pressing down hard on the Jen-Mo point immediately before ejaculation. This is an acupressure point on the perineum, halfway between the anus and scrotum. By applying the pressure correctly, the ejaculation, say the Taoists, can be reversed and the semen will then be recycled into the bloodstream and reabsorbed.

A longer orgasm

By applying this technique, the man's pleasurable sensations are greatly accentuated and since the pressure on the perineum means that orgasm happens in very slow spasms, the orgasm has the potential to continue for as long as five minutes.

SWALLOWS IN LOVE

This gentle position is inspired by the courtship
of birds. The shape that the lovers' bodies make is
reminiscent of a swallow with its forked tail. You lie
on top of your woman with your legs between hers and
your weight on your elbows. Your woman bends her

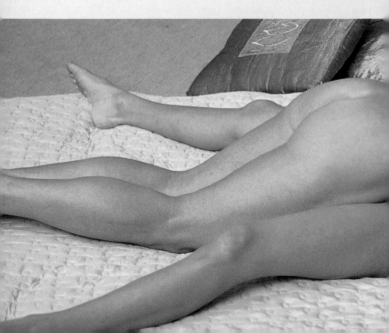

knees slightly to allow you to penetrate her. Swallows in Love offers only moderate penetration but gives lovers an opportunity to express their tenderness and enjoy a sense of togetherness. You will each experience a heightening state of arousal in this position.

SILKWORM SPINNING A COCOON

You lie on top of your woman and lean your weight onto your hands to support yourself so you can use your powerful buttock muscles to thrust. Your partner lies beneath you and crosses her ankles behind your back so she can lift and lower her hips in rhythm with your thrusts. While you thrust into your partner from this position of power, watch the pleasure and emotions on her face.

HUGE BIRD ABOVE A DARK SEA

In this position, which offers deep penetration, your partner lies on her back with her legs lifted over your arms. You lean forward against her thighs and raise her buttocks slightly so that they rest against your thighs. You then grasp her around the waist and simultaneously pull her toward you as you push into her. By lifting her legs, you change the angle of entry for your penis so that you can penetrate more deeply than in the basic missionary position.

PHOENIX PLAYING IN A RED CAVE

The imaginative title hints at the possibility of deep penetration in this position—but you should wait until your woman is fully aroused before you attempt to insert your penis. She lies on her back and holds on to her ankles to expose "the red cave" in which your penis wants to "play." Once your partner is fully aroused,

"Tao sex is said to keep a woman looking young."
THE TAO

enjoy the sexual friction of intercourse and the urge to control the action as you thrust rhythmically.

SEAGULLS ON THE WING

Your lover's wide-open knees symbolize a seagull's wings. She lies with her buttocks on the edge of the bed, her feet on the ground to support her and her legs apart. You kneel up against the side of the bed between your lover's knees and pull her toward you just enough to make penetration easy. In most man-on-top positions, the man's penis thrusts downward into the vagina, but here the penis and vagina are parallel, so for both partners the sensations feel very different and extremely exciting.

FISH

This pose is so named because your partner's movements look like the flick of a fish's tail as it darts through the water. You lie on your back with your legs extended and she lies on top of you. She moves forward a little and takes in the tip of your penis with her labia. Slowly she wiggles your penis inside her vagina (it may need manual help here). Once she has enclosed you, she moves her hips to the right and left, and up and down, in a repeated sequence. In this position your lover's breasts move sensuously against your chest as she moves to pleasure you.

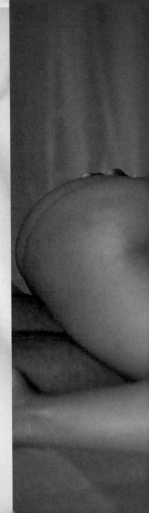

CICADA ON A BOUGH

This is a classic rear-entry position where your partner lies on her front and you stretch out along her body with your knees between hers. You push your toes against the bed as you thrust. The shape the two bodies make does, in fact, look like a cicada porched on a branch. You should try not to put too much weight onto your (usually smaller) partner's body and crush her. It may help to place a pillow under your lover's hips. This allows you even deeper penetration.

APE

This position is a traditional
favorite because it offers
you a view of your partner's
labia. As your woman lies on
her back, raises her legs up
high and rests them on your
shoulders, you kneel to lift
her up gently by the hips
and draw her sensitively
on to your penis. Make
shallow thrusts to begin
with; gradually, as the vagina
becomes moister, thrusting
can grow deeper and
stronger. The accessibility
of your lover's vagina means
that you do not have to
support your own weight,
making this an ideal position
for the older or heavier man.

PINE TREE

This is another position where your woman lies on her back with her legs raised and resting on your shoulders. The shape of her straight legs is thought to resemble a straight-growing pine tree. She holds you around the hips while, in a kneeling position, you place your hands around her waist and then penetrate her. Unlike many positions— where thrusting is left up to the intensity of desire of that moment— in this position your thrusts should be hard and fast. Because of this, the position may provide you both with a more intense physical experience than most poses.

HORSE SHAKES FEET

The Chinese consider this a playful sex position. If the woman shakes the foot of her bent leg during penetration, it gives an extra frisson to the lovemaking, but she must be careful not to knock her man over! Your woman lies on her back and places one foot up over your shoulder. She draws back the other leg close to her body so her knee is by her shoulder. If it feels comfortable, her foot can rest on your chest while you move. Kneeling upright, you penetrate your woman and thrust deeply.

DRAGON

The Dragon enables lovers to touch each other in many places and increase their feelings of intimacy. The name derives from the fact that the man, resting on his hands and knees, looks like a dragon. This mythical creature features in the names of several Taoist poses—the dragon

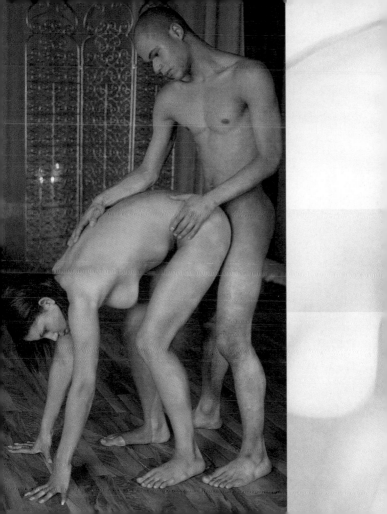

being both magical and fiery. The man lies on top of his woman with his legs between hers and his weight on his hands. He inserts his penis against the upper part of her labia and then performs the shallow and deep stroke method of thrusting known as the Sets of Nine (p.89).

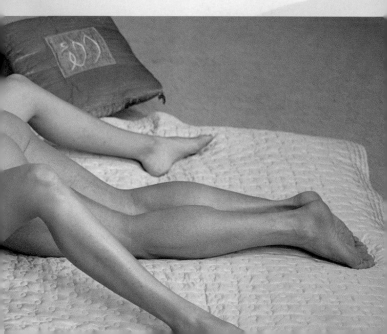

LATE SPRING DONKEY

This position is so named because it mimics the mating behavior of donkeys in springtime. Your woman bends over at the waist and, keeping her legs as straight as she can, places both hands on the floor. Holding the woman around the waist, you pull her toward your erect penis This is a playful move to be enjoyed as a game and not

"During congress, evenly stimulate the pressure points on both penis and vagina."

THE TAO

taken too seriously! Your grip on your woman's waist allows you to thrust without losing your balance and helps you to control the depth of penetration for heightened enjoyment. Ensure that she is fully aroused before you penetrate her.

MANDARIN DUCKS

This position invokes faithful affection as lovers turn their heads adoringly toward each other. There is a delightfully sensual and seductive aspect to you unexpectedly making love to your woman from the rear, especially if you are both just waking up. This position allows you to thrust easily, and, by keeping her thighs together, she can increase the pleasurable friction created by your penis inside her.

BAMBOO

Not all face-to-face love positions involve
lying down. In Bamboo we find a direct
and lustful standing posture, with the upright
bodies of the lovers resembling two bamboo
stalks. You stand facing your partner and
hold her around the waist to penetrate her.

*"An orgasm is like a flower,
uncurling from the center. "*
THE TAO

She steadies herself by leaning back on her
hands, which she places on a bed or table
behind her. As your desire increases, caress
and kiss your lover's body and mouth, or
embrace her with your arms and let your
hands roam across her back.

Index *for him*

ACKNOWLEDGEMENTS

The publisher would like to thank the following for their kind
permission to reproduce their photographs:
10-11, 38-39, 56-57: © **Christie's Images Ltd; 88-89:** © **akg-images**
All other images © Dorling Kindersley
For further information see: **www.dkimages.com**
DK would like to thank **Laurence Errington** for the index.